Card Making
With cricut™

Edited by **Tanya Fox**

Annie's Attic®

Card Making With Cricut

Copyright © 2009 DRG, 306 East Parr Road, Berne, IN 46711.

EDITOR Tanya Fox

ART DIRECTOR Brad Snow

PUBLISHING SERVICES DIRECTOR Brenda Gallmeyer

MANAGING EDITOR Barb Sprunger

ASSISTANT ART DIRECTOR Nick Pierce

COPY SUPERVISOR Michelle Beck

COPY EDITOR Amanda Ladig

TECHNICAL EDITOR Brooke Smith

PHOTOGRAPHY SUPERVISOR Tammy Christian

PHOTO STYLIST Tammy Steiner

PHOTOGRAPHY Matthew Owen

GRAPHIC ARTS SUPERVISOR Ronda Bechinski

GRAPHIC ARTIST Nicole Gage

PRODUCTION ASSISTANSTS Marj Morgan,
Judy Neuenschwander

Printed in the United States of America
First Printing: 2009
ISBN: 978-1-59635-282-7

Contents

Basic Cards

3 Busy Bee
4 Happiness Is Made …
5 Bloom
6 Baby Blessings
7 For Your Shower
8 U Rock
9 Party Hat
10 Fuzzy Bee
11 So Sweet
12 Happy Day
13 Floral Thanks
14 Butterfly Thanks
15 Have a Great Day
16 See the Flowers Smiling
17 Like a Butterfly
18 Love Life
19 Love U
20 Happy Birthday
21 Catch of the Day
22 Just a Note
23 Smile
24 It's Your Day
25 Ruff Day?
26 You Are Appreciated
27 Get Better
28 Hang in There

Unique Shape Cards

29 Owl Hello
30 You Are So Sweet
31 Sweet Girl
32 HB2U
33 4 You
34 Wishing You …
35 Special Thanks
36 For Your New Home
37 Miss You
38 Wedding Congrats
39 Love You
40 Sweet Baby Girl

Money-Holder Cards

41 Love
42 Happy Shopping
42 BIG Day
43 Thanks

Gift Card Holders

44 Teacher Gift Card
45 Super Star
46 Enjoy
47 Birthday Girl

48 Buyer's Guide

Busy Bee

Design by **Jennifer Buck**

Materials

- Cricut Expression machine
- Cartridges: Home Decor (#29-0695), Wild Card (#29-0591)
- Card stock: yellow, white, black
- Yellow Bitty Dot Basics printed paper
- 18 inches ½-inch-wide yellow satin ribbon
- Scallop-edge border punch
- Adhesive foam dots
- Paper adhesive

Form a 4¼ x 4¼-inch top-folded card from yellow card stock. Center and adhere a 4 x 4-inch piece of printed paper to card front.

Cut two 4¼ x 2¼-inch pieces of yellow card stock; punch scallops along bottom edges. Cut two 4¼ x 1⅜-inch strips of printed paper and adhere one to each scallop piece ¹⁄₁₆ inch from top edges. Adhere one piece to card front near bottom edge; adhere other piece inside card near bottom edge.

Using Wild Card cartridge, cut scallop circle. Choose 7¾-inch size on dial. Load a 12 x 12-inch piece of yellow card stock into cutter. Press "<pinwheel>," "<frame>" and "<cut>."

To cut solid circle, choose 8-inch size on dial. Load a 12 x 12-inch piece of white card stock into cutter. Press "<pinwheel>," "<liner>" and "<cut>." Adhere white circle to yellow circle. Adhere to card front as shown with foam dots.

Using Home Decor cartridge, cut bee. Choose 1¼-inch size on dial. Load a 12 x 12-inch piece of black card stock. Press "<blackout>," "<bug>" and "<cut>." Adhere to white circle. Wrap ribbon around card front below circles and tie a bow; trim ends.

Using Wild Card cartridge, cut sentiment. Choose 3½-inch size on dial. Load a 12 x 12-inch piece of black card stock into cutter. Press "<phrase>," "<quotes>" and "<cut>." Adhere to lower right corner inside card. ●

Sources: Card stock, printed paper and ribbon from Papertrey Ink; scallop-edge border punch from Stampin' Up!; Cricut machine and cartridges from Provo Craft.

thanks

Happiness Is Made . . .

Design by **Melissa Phillips**

Using Wild Card cartridge, cut birds. Choose 1½-inch size on dial. Load a 12 x 12-inch piece of yellow floral paper into cutter. Press "<shift>," "<tweety>," "<icon>" and "<cut>." Repeat once.

For small bird, choose ¾-inch size on dial. Load a 12 x 12-inch piece of yellow floral paper into cutter. Press "<shift>," "<tweety>," "<icon>" and "<cut>."

To cut sun shape, choose 2-inch size on dial. Load a 12 x 12-inch piece of off-white words paper into cutter. Press "<porthole>," "<icon>" and "<cut>."

Form a 3¾ x 5¼-inch side-folded card from yellow card stock; round right-hand corners. Cut a 3½ x 5-inch piece of orange dots paper; round right-hand corners. Ink edges. Adhere to card front aligning left edges.

Cut a 3½ x 2-inch piece of cream card stock; punch scallops along top edge. Ink edges and adhere to card front as shown ½ inch above bottom edge. Cut a 3½ x 1½-inch piece of dark pink paper; ink edges and adhere to scalloped piece. Zigzag-stitch across bottom of cream piece; straight-stitch across top of dark pink piece. Ink edges of birds and adhere across dark pink strip. Add pearls for eyes.

Cut ribbon into one 6-inch piece and one 3-inch piece. Knot ends together. Adhere near top of card front wrapping and adhering ends to back. Trim ribbon ends with pinking shears.

Cut a piece of dark pink paper to cover back of sun; adhere in place. Adhere to upper right corner of card front using foam dots. Tie buttons together with hemp cord; adhere to center of sun shape. Apply rub-on transfer below ribbon. ●

Sources: Card stock from Prism Papers; printed papers from K&Company and Graphic 45; ribbon, buttons and hemp cord from Papertrey Ink; rub-on transfer from K&Company; self-adhesive pearls from Zva Creative; scallop border punch from Fiskars; Cricut machine and cartridge from Provo Craft.

Materials

- Cricut Expression machine
- Cartridge: Wild Card (#29-059)
- Card stock: yellow, cream
- Printed papers: yellow floral, off-white words, orange dots, dark pink
- Buttons: 1 pink, 1 white
- 9 inches ⅝-inch-wide cream grosgrain ribbon
- Hemp cord
- Happiness-themed rub-on transfer
- 3 self-adhesive white pearls
- Brown ink pad
- Punches: corner rounder, scallop border
- Pinking shears
- Sewing machine with taupe thread
- Adhesive foam dots
- Paper adhesive

Bloom

Design by **Melissa Phillips**

Using Hello Kitty® Greetings cartridge, cut strawberry. Choose 3-inch size on dial. Load a 12 x 12-inch piece of red printed paper into cutter. Press "<strwbrry>," "<clothes>" and "<cut>."

To cut strawberry top, choose 3-inch size on dial. Load a 12 x 12-inch piece of green printed paper into cutter. Press "<shift>," "<strwbrry>" and "<cut>."

Materials

- Cricut Expression machine
- Cartridge: Hello Kitty® Greetings (#29-0698)
- Card stock: blue, ivory
- Printed papers: red stars, green, multicolored striped, orange dots
- "bloom" rub-on transfer
- Self-adhesive white pearls
- Large ivory button
- Brown dye ink pad
- 11 inches ⅝-inch-wide red grosgrain ribbon
- Hemp cord
- Green thread
- Scalloped border punch
- Adhesive foam dots
- Paper adhesive

Form a 3¾ x 6-inch side-folded card from blue card stock. Set aside.

Cut a 3¾ x 6-inch rectangle from blue card stock. This will be card base. Cut a 3⅜ x 5⅝-inch rectangle from ivory card stock; ink edges and adhere to blue card base.

Cut a 3⅜ x 1½-inch piece of striped paper and a 3⅜ x ¾-inch piece of orange dots paper. Punch scallops along bottom edge of orange dots piece. Ink edges of both pieces and adhere to bottom of ivory rectangle as shown. Wrap ribbon around rectangle as shown and knot on right side; trim ends in V-notches. Insert green thread through button and tie onto ribbon knot; trim ends.

Apply "bloom" rub-on transfer on left side of rectangle above striped piece. Adhere strawberry to rectangle as shown. Add pearls to strawberry. Adhere green strawberry top on top of red strawberry using foam dots. Tie a bow with hemp; trim ends and adhere to top of strawberry. Adhere assembled rectangle to card front. ●

Sources: Card stock from WorldWin Papers and Bazzill Basics Paper Inc.; printed papers from Papertrey Ink, Webster's Pages, K&Company and October Afternoon; ribbon and hemp from Papertrey Ink; rub-on transfer from BasicGrey; self-adhesive pearls from Heart & Home Inc./ Melissa Frances; scalloped border punch from Martha Stewart Crafts; Cricut machine and cartridge from Provo Craft.

Baby Blessings

Design by **Kimber McGray**

Form a 4¼ x 5½-inch side-folded card from gray card stock. Sand edges. Set aside.

- -

Using Doodlecharms cartridge, cut blue card front. Choose 5-inch size on dial. Load a 6 x 12-inch piece of printed paper into cutter. Press "<real dial size>," "<card>," "<bbyfce>" and "<cut>."

- -

For baby face, choose 1-inch size on dial. Load a 4 x 6-inch piece of peach card stock into cutter. Press "<bbyfce>" and "<cut>."

- -

For baby hair, choose 1-inch size on dial and load a 4 x 6-inch piece of brown card stock into cutter. Press "<shift>," "<bbyfce>" and "<cut>."

- -

Using Wild Card cartridge, cut sentiment. Choose 1-inch size on dial. Load a 4 x 6-inch piece of printed paper into cutter. Press "<real dial size>," "<shift>," "<carriage>" and "<cut>."

- -

To assemble card, tie ribbon around top of blue polka-dot card front and tie a bow. Trim ribbon ends. Adhere to card base with foam tape. Adhere baby face with two layers of foam tape. Adhere hair to top of baby face. Add pearls to card front. Adhere sentiment inside card. ●

Sources: Gray and brown card stock from Core'dinations; peach card stock from WorldWin Papers; printed paper from Jillibean Soup; ribbon from Creative Impressions; pearls from Zva Creative; Cricut machine and cartridges from Provo Craft.

Materials

- Cricut machine
- Cartridges: Doodlecharms (#29-0021), Wild Card (#29-0591)
- Card stock: gray, brown, peach
- Soup Staples Light Blue Sugar double-sided printed paper
- 18 inches 1-inch-wide white satin ribbon
- Self-adhesive white pearls
- Sandpaper
- Adhesive foam tape
- Paper adhesive

For Your Shower

Design by **Melissa Phillips**

Materials

- Cricut Expression machine
- Cartridge: New Arrival (#29-0222)
- Dark turquoise/turquoise double-sided card stock
- Printed papers: blue dots, white/blue floral, green
- White printed vellum
- 16 inches ⅝-inch-wide white grosgrain ribbon
- Clear flat-back gems
- Clear glitter
- White paper flowers
- 3¼ inches white lace trim
- Corner rounder
- Pinking shears
- Sewing machine with white thread
- Adhesive dimensional dots
- Paper adhesive

Using New Arrival cartridge, cut bottom umbrella. Choose 3½-inch size on dial. Load a 12 x 12-inch piece of blue dots printed paper into cutter. Press "<shadow>," "<umbrella>" and "<cut>."

To cut top umbrella, choose 3¼-inch size on dial. Load a 12 x 12-inch piece of white/blue floral printed paper into cutter. Press "<shift>," "<shadow>," "<umbrella>" and "<cut>."

To cut sentiment, choose ¾-inch size on dial. Load a 12 x 12-inch piece of blue dots printed paper into cutter. Press"<babyshwr>," "<shift>," "<shadow>" and "<cut>."

Form a 4¼ x 5-inch top-folded card from dark turquoise card stock. Round bottom corners on card front only. Cut a 3⅞ x 4¾-inch piece of green printed paper and adhere to card front aligning top edges. Cut a 3⅞ x 3-inch piece of vellum; adhere to card aligning top edges. Machine-sew zigzag stitches along top of card front. Wrap ribbon around card front along bottom of vellum and tie a bow on left side; trim ends with pinking shears.

Adhere lace trim along underside at bottom of bottom umbrella; trim edges even. Adhere top umbrella on top of bottom umbrella using dimensional dots. Adhere to card front as shown. Cover "Shower" with glitter and adhere to bottom of card front. Embellish umbrella and "Shower" with flowers and gems. ●

Sources: Card stock and printed papers from SEI; vellum and ribbon from Papertrey Ink; gems and glitter from Doodlebug Design Inc.; paper flowers and trim from Making Memories; Cricut machine and cartridge from Provo Craft.

U Rock

Design by **Lynn Ghahary**

Using Indie Art cartridge, cut a guitar. Choose 4-inch size on dial. Load a 4 x 6-inch piece of white card stock into cutter. Press "<shadow>," "<guitar1>" and "<cut>."

To cut another guitar, choose 4-inch size on dial. Load a 4 x 6-inch piece of brown card stock into cutter. Press "<guitar1>" and "<cut>." Repeat with Patchwork paper, orange side up.

Using Tags, Bags, Boxes & More cartridge, cut tag. Choose 5-inch size on dial. Load a 6 x 6-inch piece of Camo paper into cutter. Press "<blackout>," "<bvltop>" and "<cut>."

Using Plantin SchoolBook cartridge, cut circle. Choose 1-inch size on dial. Load a 4 x 6-inch piece of Patchwork paper, orange side up, into cutter. Press "<shadow>," "<circle>" and "<cut>."

To cut a star, choose 1-inch size on dial. Load a 4 x 6-inch piece of Patchwork paper that includes orange star on it into cutter. Press "<star>" and "<cut>."

To cut "U", choose 5-inch size on dial. Load a 6 x 6-inch piece of Patchwork paper, orange side up, into cutter. Press "<shadow>," "<U>" and "<cut>."

Using Street Sign cartridge, cut "rock." Choose 1¼-inch size on dial. Load a 6 x 6-inch piece of Star paper into cutter. Press "<r>," "<o>," "<c>" and "<k>" and "<cut>."

Form a 4½ x 5¾-inch side-folded card from kraft card stock. Cut a 4¼ x 5½-inch rectangle from Star paper; distress edges. Machine-stitch along edges. Center and adhere to card front.

Adhere orange circle to top of camo tag; punch a ⅛-inch hole through center of circle. Thread hemp cord through hole; trim ends. Adhere tag to card front as shown. Staple end of cord to card front.

Adhere orange guitar body to brown guitar. Adhere brown guitar to white guitar. Adhere guitar to tag on card front. Adhere orange star to upper right corner of card front. Adhere crystal star and gems to card front as shown.

Adhere orange "U" inside card. Adhere "rock" inside card on top of "U." ●

Sources: Card stock from Bazzill Basics Paper Inc.; printed papers from Making Memories; crystal star from Kaisercraft; self-adhesive gems from me & my BIG ideas; Cricut machine and cartridges from Provo Craft.

Materials

- Cricut Expression machine
- Cartridges: Plantin SchoolBook (#29-0390), Indie Art (#29-0539), Street Sign (#29-0547), Tags, Bags, Boxes & More (#29-0022)
- Card stock: brown, kraft, white
- Just Chillin double-sided printed papers: Camo, Star, Patchwork
- Self-adhesive gems
- Self-adhesive crystal star
- Hemp cord
- Stapler
- ⅛-inch hole punch
- Sewing machine with white thread
- Paper adhesive

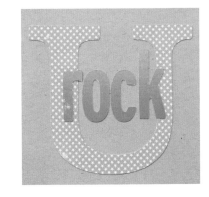

Party Hat

Design by **Kimber McGray**

Materials
- Cricut machine
- Cartridges: Doodlecharms (#29-0021), Wild Card (#29-0591)
- Card stock: red, light blue
- Double-sided printed papers: Soup Staples Navy Sugar, Soup Staples Light Blue Sugar, Alphabet Soup Vegetable Juice
- Numbers ribbon
- Scallop border punch
- Sandpaper
- Adhesive foam tape
- Paper adhesive

Form a 5½ x 4¼-inch top-folded card from Navy Sugar paper. Set aside.

Using Doodlecharms cartridge, cut striped portion of party hat. Choose 4-inch size on dial and load a 6 x 12-inch piece of Vegetable Juice paper into cutter. Press "<shift>," "<hat>" and "<cut>."

For blue top of party hat, choose a 4-inch size on dial and load a 4 x 6-inch piece of Light Blue Sugar paper into cutter. Press "<shift>," "<hat>" and "<cut>."

For red shadow portion of party hat, choose 4-inch size on dial and load a 6 x 12-inch piece of red card stock into cutter. Press "<shadow>," "<hat>" and "<cut>." Sand edges.

Using Wild Card cartridge, cut "Happy Birthday" sentiment. Choose 2½-inch size on dial. Load a 6 x 6-inch piece of light blue card stock into cutter. Press "<real dial size>," "<phrase>," "<cupcake>" and "<cut>."

To assemble card, use scallop border punch to punch bottom edge of a 5½ x 1¼-inch piece of Light Blue Sugar paper. Adhere near bottom of card front. Wrap ribbon around card front as shown; knot on right side. Trim ends. Adhere red hat shadow to left side of card with foam tape. Adhere striped hat to card front with foam tape. Adhere blue pompom to top of hat. Cut a 4 x 5¼-inch rectangle from red card stock; sand edges. Adhere inside card. Adhere sentiment inside card. ●

Sources: Card stock from Core'dinations; printed papers and ribbon from Jillibean Soup; punch from Stampin' Up!; Cricut machine and cartridges from Provo Craft.

Fuzzy Bee

Design by **Jennifer Buck**

Form a 5 x 5½-inch top-folded card from kraft card stock. Cut two 2 x 2-inch squares, one from each printed paper. Cut one 2 x ¾-inch strip from Sunday paper. Referring to photo, adhere squares and strip to card front. Hand-sew random stitches on paper pieces.

Using Walk in My Garden cartridge, cut bee. Choose 2-inch size on dial. Load a 12 x 12-inch piece of yellow card stock into cutter. Press "<bee>" and "<cut>." Repeat once more with yellow card stock and once with black card stock. Layer pieces as shown and adhere. Flip up wings. Apply Flower Soft Glue and add sprinkles to bee. Let dry. Adhere to card front as shown with foam tape. Pierce a swirl of dots behind bee with sewing needle. Wrap ribbon around top of card front and tie a bow; trim ends.

Adhere a 5 x ⅝-inch strip of Saturday paper near bottom of a 5 x 1¾-inch strip of Sunday paper. Adhere inside card ⅜ inch above bottom edge. Adhere a 2½ x 2½-inch piece of ivory card stock inside card along bottom edge as shown.

Using Wild Card cartridge, cut sentiment. Choose 5-inch size on dial. Load a 12 x 12-inch piece of black card stock inside cutter. Press "<phrase>," "<oval>" and "<cut>." Adhere to ivory square inside card. ●

Sources: Card stock from Stampin' Up!; printed papers from Cosmo Cricket; ribbon from Papertrey Ink; colored sprinkles and Flower Soft Glue from Flower Soft Inc.; Cricut machine and cartridges from Provo Craft.

Materials

- Cricut Expression machine
- Cartridges: Walk in My Garden (#29-0223), Wild Card (#29-0591)
- Card stock: kraft, yellow, black, ivory
- Girl Friday double-sided printed papers: Saturday, Sunday
- Black colored sprinkles
- 20 inches ⅝-inch-wide black grosgrain ribbon
- Black thread
- Sewing needle
- Flower Soft Glue
- Adhesive foam tape
- Paper adhesive

So Sweet

Design by **Kandis Smith**

Materials

- Cricut Expression machine
- Cartridge: Walk in My Garden (#29-0223)
- Card stock: red, white, black
- Printed papers: black lines, light green, red polka-dot
- "so sweet!" stamp
- Red ink pad
- Red brad
- Small red button
- 20 inches jute
- Gold glitter
- Sandpaper
- Piercing tool
- Scallop border punch
- Sewing machine with brown thread
- Adhesive foam dots
- Paper adhesive

Form a 5½ x 5½-inch top-folded card from red card stock; sand edges. Adhere a 3¾ x 5½-inch piece of black lines printed paper to card front ¼ inch from left edge.

Cut a 5½ x 1-inch strip of white card stock; punch scallops along edge. Adhere to back of a 5½ x 3¼-inch piece of light green printed paper along bottom edge. Adhere to card front as shown. Machine-sew zigzag stitches along top of green piece; straight-stitch along bottom edge. Wrap jute around card front and tie a bow on right side; trim ends. Adhere button to center of bow.

Cut a 1⅞-inch circle from white card stock; cut in half. Stamp "so sweet!" on one half. Adhere to upper left area of card front as shown. Pierce a hole through top of half-circle and insert brad.

Using Walk in My Garden cartridge, cut ladybug. Choose 4-inch size on dial. Load a 12 x 12-inch piece of black card stock into cutter. Press "<ladybug>" and "<cut>."

To cut a second ladybug, choose 4-inch size on dial. Load a 12 x 12-inch piece of red polka-dot printed paper into cutter. Press "<shift>," "<ladybug>" and "<cut>." Layer pieces as shown and adhere. Add glitter to ladybug. Adhere to card front with foam dots. ●

Sources: Card stock from Core'dinations; printed papers from American Crafts Inc. and Kaisercraft; stamps from Hero Arts; brads from Making Memories; Cricut machine and cartridge from Provo Craft.

Happy Day

Design by **Kandis Smith**

Project note: *Sand edges as desired.*

Form a 4½ x 7½-inch side-folded card from blue card stock. Cut and adhere a 4 x 7⅛-inch piece of orange card stock to card front. Cut a 3¾ x 7-inch piece of white words/green paper with zigzags along bottom. Adhere a 3¾ x 2½-inch piece of orange floral paper near bottom of zigzag paper. Wrap ribbon around top of rectangle and tie a bow on left side; trim ribbon ends at an angle. Adhere to card front. Machine-sew zigzag stitches along top of white/green rectangle and along top of orange floral piece. Tie thread through button; adhere to ribbon bow with adhesive dot. Stamp "happy day" below bow.

Using Walk in My Garden cartridge, cut snail. Choose 3-inch size on dial. Load a 12 x 12-inch piece of green card stock into cutter. Press "<snail>" and "<cut>." To cut snail shell, choose 3-inch size on dial. Load a 12 x 12-inch piece of yellow card stock into cutter. Press "<shift>," "<snail>" and "<cut>." Adhere snail shell to snail as shown. Add glitter and adhere to card front. ●

Sources: Card stock from Core'dinations; printed papers from Making Memories; stamp from Hero Arts; glitter from Ranger Industries Inc.; Cricut machine and cartridge from Provo Craft.

Materials

- Cricut Expression machine
- Cartridge: Walk in My Garden (#29-0223)
- Card stock: blue, green, orange, yellow
- Printed papers: orange floral, white words/green zigzag-edged
- "happy day" stamp
- Blue dye ink pad
- 15 inches ⅝-inch-wide green satin ribbon
- Clear glitter
- Orange round button
- White thread
- Sandpaper
- Sewing machine with orange thread
- Adhesive dot
- Paper adhesive

Floral Thanks

Design by **Kandis Smith**

Form a 6 x 6-inch side-folded card from yellow card stock. Center and adhere a 5½ x 5½-inch piece of orange polka-dot paper to card front. Machine-stitch along edges of paper.

Using Accent Essentials cartridge, cut frame. Choose 4-inch size on dial. Load a 12 x 12-inch piece of blue card stock into cutter. Press "<frame outline>" and "<cut>."

To cut frame backing, choose 4-inch size on dial. Load a 12 x 12-inch piece of green printed paper. Press "<shift>," "<frame outline>" and "<cut>." Adhere blue frame on top of frame background leaving inside edges of frame free of adhesive. Adhere to card as shown; trim edges even.

Cut a 2 x 4¼-inch piece of orange floral paper and machine-stitch along side edges. Adhere centered inside frame sliding bottom edge underneath bottom edge of frame. Pierce a hole on each side of frame and insert brads. Stamp flourish on right side of card front with green ink.

Using Walk in My Garden cartridge, cut flowers. Choose 2-inch size on dial. Load a 12 x 12-inch piece of yellow card stock into cutter. Press "<six petal flower>" and "<cut>." Repeat four more times, twice changing dial size to ½ inch and twice changing dial size to ¼ inch.

To cut daisy, choose 1¾-inch size on dial. Load a 12 x 12-inch piece of blue card stock into cutter. Press "<daisy>" and "<cut>."

To cut leaves, choose 1-inch size on dial. Load a 12 x 12-inch piece of green card stock into cutter. Press "<leaf>" and "<cut>."

Punch a flower from orange polka-dot paper. Layer and adhere following flowers: orange, blue and large yellow. Sand flowers and leaves. Adhere leaves and layered flower to center bottom of frame. Adhere remaining flowers to card front as shown; add pearls to centers of small flowers.

Tie string through button; trim ends. Adhere to center of orange flower. Stamp "thanks" onto kraft card stock with orange ink; cut a 3 x 1-inch rectangle around word placing word on right side; round right end. Adhere to card front as shown. Adhere inside edges of frame. ●

Materials

- Cricut Expression machine
- Cartridges: Walk in My Garden (#29-0223), Accent Essentials (#29-0391)
- Card stock: yellow, blue, green, kraft
- Printed papers: orange polka-dot, green, orange floral
- Stamps: flourish, "Thanks"
- Ink pads: green, orange
- White self-adhesive pearls
- 2 metal brads
- Yellow button
- Punches: corner rounder, small flower
- 3 inches linen string
- Sandpaper
- Piercing tool
- Sewing machine with brown thread
- Paper adhesive

Sources: Card stock from Core'dinations; printed papers from Making Memories; stamp and pearls from Hero Arts; Cricut machine and cartridges from Provo Craft.

Butterfly Thanks

Design by **Kandis Smith**

Form a 4 x 6-inch top-folded card from pink printed paper. Cut a 3½ x 5⅝-inch piece of green printed paper; add photo corners to bottom corners. Adhere to card front aligning top edges. Machine-sew zigzag stitches at top of rectangle.

Emboss dots onto a 4 x 2¼-inch piece of yellow card stock; sand and adhere to center of card front. Cut a 2⅞-inch circle from green printed paper; adhere to center of embossed strip. Wrap ribbon around card front and tie a bow on right side; trim ends. Use an adhesive dot to adhere button to ribbon bow.

Using Walk in My Garden cartridge, cut butterfly. Choose 2½-inch size on dial. Load a 12 x 12-inch piece of floral paper into cutter. Press "<butterfly>" and "<cut>."

To cut butterfly details, choose 1½-inch size on dial. Load a 12 x 12-inch piece of printed paper into cutter. Press "<shift>," "<butterfly>" and "<cut>." Repeat for each color of printed paper you desire for butterfly details.

To cut sentiment, choose 2½-inch size on dial. Load a 12 x 12-inch piece of pink printed paper into cutter. Press "<sentiment thanks>" and "<cut>."

Adhere butterfly details to floral butterfly. Add glitter to butterfly. Adhere to card front as shown. Adhere sentiment to bottom of card. ●

Sources: Card stock from Core'dinations; printed papers from BasicGrey; button from Dress It Up; glitter from Ranger Industries Inc.; stamps from Hero Arts; Cricut machine and cartridge, and Cuttlebug embossing machine and embossing folder from Provo Craft.

Materials

- Cricut Expression machine
- Cartridge: Walk in My Garden (#29-0223)
- Yellow card stock
- Printed papers: pink, green, blue, floral
- 2 gold photo corners
- 16 inches ⅝-inch-wide turquoise satin ribbon
- Silver decorative button
- Clear glitter
- Sandpaper
- Sewing machine with brown thread
- Swiss Dots embossing folder (#37-1604)
- Embossing machine
- Adhesive dot
- Paper adhesive

Have a Great Day

Design by **Kandis Smith**

Form a 4¾ x 7-inch side-folded card from gray card stock; round right-hand corners. Sand edges. Cut a 4¼ x 6½-inch piece of olive green card stock; round right-hand corners. Sand edges. Adhere to card front. Cut a 4¾ x 1¾-inch piece of orange card stock; sand edges and adhere to card front 1¾ inches above bottom edge. Machine-sew zigzag stitches along left edge of olive green piece; straight-stitch across bottom of orange piece.

Stamp "have a GREAT DAY" on right side of a 2½ x 1-inch piece of pink card stock; sand and place on left side of orange piece. Punch a ¹⁄₁₆-inch hole through left end of sentiment rectangle and insert brad.

Using Walk in My Garden cartridge, cut large flowers. Choose 3-inch size on dial. Load a 12 x 12-inch piece of floral paper into cutter. Press "<pointy petal flower>" and "<cut>." Repeat with gray card stock.

To cut medium flowers, choose 2½-inch size on dial. Load a 12 x 12-inch piece of floral paper into cutter. Press "<shift>," "<pointy petal flower>" and "<cut>." Repeat with gray card stock.

To cut small flowers, choose 2-inch size on dial. Load a 12 x 12-inch piece of floral paper into cutter. Press "<shift>," "<pointy petal flower>" and "<cut>." Repeat with gray card stock.

Layer and adhere flowers together as shown. Tie thread through buttons tying a bow on front of red button. Trim thread ends. Adhere to flower centers with adhesive dots. Adhere flowers to card front. ●

Materials
- Cricut Expression machine
- Cartridge: Walk in My Garden (#29-0223)
- Card stock: gray, olive green, orange, pink
- Various floral printed papers
- "have a GREAT DAY" stamp
- Red ink pad
- Buttons: 1 red, 1 green, 1 orange
- Linen thread
- Silver brad
- Sandpaper
- Punches: corner rounder, ¹⁄₁₆-inch hole
- Sewing machine with brown thread
- Adhesive dots
- Paper adhesive

Sources: Card stock from Core'dinations; printed papers from K&Company; stamp from Hero Arts; buttons from Dress It Up and Hero Arts; Cricut machine and cartridge from Provo Craft.

See the Flowers Smiling

Design by **Kandis Smith**

Form a 4½ x 7½-inch side-folded card from blue card stock. Cut a 4 x 7-inch piece of white lined paper; attach photo corners to top corners. Adhere to card front. Adhere a 4 x 3-inch piece of polka-dot paper to bottom of lined paper on card front.

Cut a 4 x 1-inch piece of pink printed paper; adhere a 4 x 1-inch piece of orange card stock to back of pink strip along bottom edge. Punch scallops along bottom of orange piece. Sand edges of scallops. Adhere to card front as shown. Do not apply adhesive to scallops. Machine-stitch along top and bottom of pink strip.

Pierce a hole through card fold next to pink strip. Thread jute through hole; wrap jute around card front and tie a bow on front. Trim ends.

Stamp sentiment on kraft card stock; cut a square around words and adhere to left side of card sliding top edge underneath scallops.

Using Walk in My Garden cartridge, cut four flower bases. Choose 1-inch size on dial. Load a 12 x 12-inch piece of light green card stock into cutter. Press "<tulip>" and "<cut>."

To cut flower tops, choose 1-inch size on dial. Load a 12 x 12-inch piece of red card stock into cutter. Press "<shift>," "<tulip>" and "<cut>." Repeat with pink, yellow and red card stock to make a total of eight flowers. Adhere flowers to tops of green flower bases. Adhere to card as shown leaving tops of flowers free of adhesive. Add glitter to flowers. ●

Sources: Card stock from Core'dinations; printed papers from BasicGrey and SEI; stamp from Hero Arts; glitter from Ranger Industries Inc.; Cricut machine and cartridge from Provo Craft.

Materials

- Cricut Expression machine
- Cartridge: Walk in My Garden (#29-0223)
- Card stock: blue, orange, kraft, light green, red, pink, yellow
- Printed papers: white lined, polka-dot, pink
- 2 brown photo corners
- 18 inches jute
- Clear glitter
- Flower-themed sentiment stamp
- Red ink pad
- Sandpaper
- Piercing tool
- Scallop border punch
- Sewing machine with brown thread
- Paper adhesive

Like a Butterfly

Design by **Lynn Ghahary**

Materials

- Cricut Expression machine
- Cartridge: Home Decor (#29-0695)
- Kraft card stock
- Printed papers: blue, green, pink, white, striped
- White vellum
- Self-adhesive white pearls
- Black fine-tip pen
- Corner rounder
- Craft knife
- Paper adhesive
- Computer and printer (optional)

Using Home Decor cartridge, cut butterfly. Choose 3-inch size on dial. Load a 6 x 12-inch piece of pink printed paper into cutter. Press "<buttrfly>" and "<cut>."

To cut butterfly shadow, choose 3-inch size on dial. Load a 6 x 12-inch piece of blue printed paper into cutter. Press "<shadow>," "<buttrfly>" and "<cut>."

To cut circle frame, choose 3½-inch size on dial. Load a 6 x 12-inch piece of green printed paper into cutter. Press "<circlfrm>" and "<cut>."

To cut inside sentiment, choose 2½-inch size on dial. Load a 6 x 12-inch piece of pink printed paper into cutter. Press "<shadow>," "<love>" and "<cut>."

Form a 7 x 4½-inch top-folded card from kraft card stock. Round corners. Cut a 6¾ x 2½-inch piece of white printed paper; round top corners. Adhere to card front ⅛ inch below top edge. Cut a 7 x 2-inch piece of striped paper. Place green circle frame centered along top edge of striped piece and use craft knife to trim striped paper away from inside green frame. Adhere frame and striped paper to card front as shown. Trim edges even.

Adhere pink butterfly to blue butterfly shadow, and adhere centered inside green frame. Add pearls.

For inside, hand-print, or use a computer to generate, "is like a butterfly: It goes where it pleases and it pleases wherever it goes. ~Author Unknown" onto vellum. Trim a 6¾ x 4⅛-inch rectangle around sentiment leaving room above sentiment for "love." Round corners and adhere inside card with vellum adhesive. Attach pearls to corners. Adhere "love" above sentiment. ●

Sources: Card stock from Bazzill Basics Paper Inc.; printed papers from BasicGrey; vellum from Stampin' Up!; self-adhesive pearls from Zva Creative; Cricut machine and cartridge from Provo Craft.

Love Life

Design by **Melissa Phillips**

Using Wild Card cartridge, cut argyle image. Choose 3-inch size on dial. Load a 12 x 12-inch piece of pink card stock into cutter. Press "<argyle>," "<icon>" and "<cut>."

Using Beyond Birthdays cartridge, cut love sentiment. Choose ¾-inch size on dial. Load a 12 x 12-inch piece of black printed paper into cutter. Press "<love>," "<icon>" and "<cut>."

Form a 4½ x 4½-inch side-folded card from ivory card stock; ink edges. Cut a 4¼ x 4¼-inch piece of pink printed paper; ink edges and adhere to card front. Cut a 3¾ x 3¾-inch piece of light blue printed paper; ink edges and adhere to card front.

Cut a 3¾ x 1-inch piece of green printed paper; ink edges. Adhere cream trim to reverse side of green strip along bottom edge. Adhere just above bottom edge of light blue printed paper. Machine-sew zigzag stitches along top of green strip and along top of light blue paper.

Apply glitter over entire argyle piece. Cut a piece of sheet music to fit behind argyle piece; adhere in place. Adhere to card front as shown. Ink edges of chipboard star and adhere overlapping argyle piece. Adhere flower to star. Tie buttons together with hemp cord; adhere to flower center. Adhere "love" at bottom of argyle piece. Attach stickers to lower right corner of card to spell "life." ●

Sources: Card stock from Bazzill Basics Paper Inc. and WorldWin Papers; printed papers from BasicGrey and Heart & Home Inc./Melissa Frances; stickers from Making Memories; chipboard star from Heart & Home Inc./Melissa Frances; glitter from Doodlebug Design Inc.; buttons and hemp cord from Papertrey Ink; Cricut machine and cartridges from Provo Craft.

Materials

- Cricut Expression machine
- Cartridges: Wild Card (#29-0591), Beyond Birthdays (#29-0024)
- Card stock: pink, ivory
- Printed papers: black, pink, light blue, green
- Old sheet music
- Alphabet stickers
- Chipboard star
- 3¾ inches cream decorative trim
- White glitter
- Brown ink pad
- Ivory silk flower
- Buttons: 1 pink, 1 white
- Hemp cord
- Sewing machine with taupe thread
- Paper adhesive

Love U

Design by Jennifer Buck

Form a 4¼ x 5½-inch top-folded card from pale pink card stock. Center and adhere a 4 x 5¼-inch piece of Love Blooms paper to card front.

Cut two 4¼ x 2¼-inch pieces of light blue card stock; punch scallops along top edge of each. Cut two 4¼ x 1¾-inch pieces of light blue polka-dot paper; adhere one to each scallop piece. Adhere one piece to card front 1 inch above bottom edge. Adhere other piece inside card 1 inch above bottom edge. Wrap ribbon around card front along bottom of scallop piece and tie a bow; trim ends.

Using Fabulous Finds cartridge, cut clipboard. Choose 3-inch size on dial. Load a 12 x 12-inch piece of brown card stock into cutter. Press "<shift>," "<clipbrd2>" and "<cut>." Repeat with a 12 x 12-inch piece of silver card stock. Adhere silver top to brown clipboard. Adhere to card front as shown using dimensional dots.

To cut clipboard paper, choose 3-inch size on dial. Load a 12 x 12-inch piece of white card stock into cutter. Press "<shift>," "<inserts>," "<clipbrd2>" and "<cut>." Adhere to brown clipboard.

To cut "♥", choose 1½-inch size on dial. Load a 12 x 12-inch piece of dark pink card stock into cutter. Press "<shift>," "<inserts>," "<charm2>" and "<cut>." Adhere to left side of clipboard. Tie twine through small button; knot on top and trim ends. Adhere on top of heart.

Using Lyrical Letters cartridge, cut "u." Choose 1½-inch size on dial. Load a 12 x 12-inch piece of black card stock into cutter. Press "<u>" and "<cut>." Adhere to clipboard as shown.

Thread twine through large button and tie into a bow; trim ends. Adhere to lower right corner inside card. ●

Sources: Card stock, Bitty Dot Basics paper, ribbon, twine and button from Papertrey Ink; Love Blooms paper from Adornit/Carolee's Creations; scallop border punch from Stampin' Up!; Cricut machine and cartridges from Provo Craft.

Materials

- Cricut Expression machine
- Cartridges: Fabulous Finds (#29-0286), Lyrical Letters (#29-0708)
- Card stock: pale pink, light blue, white, brown, black, dark pink, silver
- Printed papers: Love Blooms, light blue Bitty Dot Basics
- 16 inches ½-inch-wide light blue satin ribbon
- Light blue buttons: 1 large, 1 small
- Twine
- Scallop border punch
- Adhesive dimensional dots
- Paper adhesive

Happy Birthday

Design by **Kimber McGray**

Materials

- Cricut Expression machine
- Cartridge: ZooBalloo (#29-0225)
- Double-sided printed papers:
  Lil' Buddy Bundle,
  Lil' Miss Sugar

Using ZooBalloo cartridge, choose 4¼-inch size on dial. Load a 12 x 12-inch piece of printed paper into cutter. Press "<card>," "<hppybday>" and "<cut>." Fold in half.

To cut envelope, choose 4¼-inch size on dial. Continue on 12 x 12-inch piece of printed paper. Press "<shift>," "<lower/layer>," "<card>" and "<cut>." Assemble envelope. ●

Sources: Printed papers from Pebbles Inc.; Cricut machine and cartridge from Provo Craft.

Catch of the Day

Design by **Kimber McGray**

Materials

- Cricut machine
- Cartridge: Wild Card (#29-0591)
- Printed papers: Lentil Soup Ground Coriander, Lentil Soup Kosher Salt, Brown Pea Pod
- Light brown chalk ink pad
- Twine
- Adhesive foam tape
- Paper adhesive

Using Wild Card cartridge, cut card base. Choose 5½-inch size on dial and load a 6 x 12-inch piece of Brown Pea Pod paper into cutter. Press "<father>" and "<cut>."

For fish, choose 5½-inch size on dial. Load a 6 x 6-inch piece of Kosher Salt paper into cutter. Press "<icon>," "<shift>," "<father>" and "<cut>."

For green paisley frame, choose 5½-inch size on dial. Load a 6 x 12-inch piece of Ground Coriander paper into cutter. Press "<liner>," "<father>" and "<cut>." Save center square scrap.

For "Celebrate" sentiment, choose 5½-inch size on dial. Load a 6 x 6-inch piece of Ground Coriander paper into cutter. Press "<shift>," "<phrase>," "<star>" and "<cut>."

To assemble card, ink all edges. Adhere green frame to card base with foam tape. Tie twine around raised frame at top. Hook fish in twine. Adhere green square scrap from frame to reverse side of card front covering hole. Adhere sentiment inside card. ●

Sources: Printed papers and twine from Jillibean Soup; chalk ink pad from Clearsnap Inc.; Cricut machine and cartridge from Provo Craft.

Just a Note

Design by **Kimber McGray**

Using Wild Card cartridge, cut flower card base. Choose 4-inch size on dial. Load a 12 x 12-inch piece of Apron Strings paper into cutter. Press "<flower>" and "<cut>."

- -

To cut flower shadow, choose 4¼-inch size on dial. Load a 6 x 12-inch piece of Ribbon Sandwich paper into cutter. Press "<frame>," "<flower>" and "<cut>."

- -

To cut Just a Note sentiment, choose 4-inch size on dial. Continue using same piece of printed paper. Press "<phrase>," "<shift>," "<flower>" and "<cut>."

- -

Score and fold card. Place blue flower shadow behind card front and trim edges of two petals to fit; adhere blue flower shadow to back of card front. Adhere button to flower center.

- -

Adhere a 3⅝ x 3½-inch piece of Sunrise paper inside card. Adhere sentiment to left side inside card. ●

Sources: Printed papers from Cosmo Cricket; button from Making Memories; Cricut machine and cartridge from Provo Craft.

Materials

- Cricut Expression machine
- Cartridge: Wild Card (#29-0591)
- Early Bird double-sided printed papers: Apron Strings, Ribbon Sandwich, Sunrise
- Blue button
- Paper adhesive

Smile

Design by **Kimber McGray**

Cut a 4¼ x 12-inch piece of printed paper. Round corners. With short side horizontal, score horizontal lines 1½ inches from bottom edge and 5 inches from top edge; fold bottom flap up and top flap down. Staple bottom of bottom flap to hold.

Using Wild Card cartridge, cut smiley face. Choose 2½-inch size on dial. Load a 6 x 12-inch piece of yellow card stock into cutter. Press "<icon>," "<real dial size>," "<triangle>" and "<cut>."

To cut smile sentiment, choose 1¼-inch size on dial. Load a 6 x 12-inch piece of yellow card stock into cutter. Press "<phrase>," "<real dial size>," "<triangle>" and "<cut>."

To cut inside sentiment, choose 2½-inch size on dial. Load a 6 x 12-inch piece of yellow card stock into cutter. Press "<phrase>," "<shift>," "<real dial size>," "<thinking>" and "<cut>."

To cut heart, choose 1-inch size on dial. Load a 4 x 6-inch piece of pink card stock. Press "<liner>," "<real dial size>," <heart> and "<cut>."

Adhere smiley face and "smile" to card front with foam dots. Wrap ribbon around bottom flap and tie a knot; trim ends. Adhere sentiment inside card. Adhere heart above sentiment with foam dots. ●

Sources: Card stock from Core'dinations; printed paper from Making Memories; ribbon from BasicGrey; Cricut machine and cartridge from Provo Craft.

Materials
- Cricut Expression machine
- Cartridge: Wild Card (#29-0591)
- Card stock: yellow, pink
- Just Chillin Girl Multistripe double-sided printed paper
- 12 inches ½-inch-wide pink stitched ribbon
- Corner rounder
- Stapler
- Adhesive foam dots
- Paper adhesive

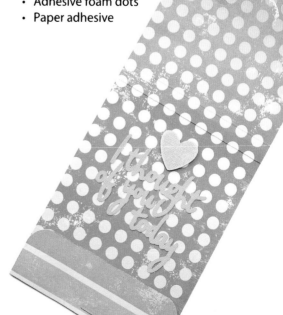

It's Your Day

Design by **Jennifer Buck**

Cut a 4¼ x 11-inch piece of kraft card stock. With short side horizontal, score horizontal lines 2½ inches from top edge and 3 inches from bottom edge. Fold up bottom flap; fold down top flap.

Cut a 4¼ x 2¾-inch piece of olive green card stock; punch scallops along bottom edge. Adhere to reverse side of top flap. Using needle and white thread, hand-sew zigzag stitches along edge of top flap where kraft card stock meets with olive green card stock.

Adhere a 4 x 5¼-inch piece of Love paper inside card. Using Accent Essentials cartridge, cut a scallop square. Choose 3¼-inch size on dial. Load a 12 x 12-inch piece of olive green card stock into cutter. Press "<shadow>," "<shift>," "<accnt47s>" and "<cut>." Center and adhere a 2¾ x 2¾-inch piece of ivory card stock to scallop square. Adhere inside card.

Using George and Basic Shapes cartridge, cut "IT'S YOUR DAY" sentiment. Choose 3¼-inch size on dial. Load a 12 x 12-inch piece of black card stock into cutter. Press "<shadow>," "<it's your day>" and "<cut>." Adhere to ivory square using a glue pen.

To cut flower, choose 2½-inch size on dial. Load a 12 x 12-inch piece of yellow card stock into cutter. Press "<shadow blackout>," "<shift>," "<flower2>" and "<cut>." Change dial size to 2¼ inch and repeat with a 12 x 12-inch piece of My Friend paper to cut a smaller flower.

Layer flowers and adhere to top flap as shown using dimensional dots. Punch a ¾-inch circle from Love paper. Adhere to flower center. Thread twine through button and knot on top; trim ends. Adhere to flower center slightly off-center. ●

Sources: Card stock and scallop border punch from Stampin' Up!; printed papers from My Mind's Eye; button and twine from Papertrey Ink; Cricut machine and cartridges from Provo Craft.

Materials

- Cricut Expression machine
- Cartridges: George and Basic Shapes (#29-0025), Accent Essentials (#29-0391)
- Card stock: kraft, olive green, ivory, black, yellow
- Penny Lane Free Bird double-sided printed papers: Love words, My Friend brown/red
- Blue round button
- Twine
- White thread
- Sewing needle
- Punches: scallop border, ¾-inch circle
- Glue pen
- Adhesive dimensional dots
- Paper adhesive

Materials

- Cricut Expression machine
- Cartridges: Doodlecharms (#29-0021), Plantin SchoolBook (#29-0390), Lyrical Letters (#29-0708)
- Card stock: kraft, brown, red, ivory
- Printed papers: Lentil Soup Kosher Salt, Lentil Soup Vegetable Broth
- 4½ inches brown decorative trim
- 2 googly eyes
- Stapler
- Adhesive foam dots
- Paper adhesive

Ruff Day?

Design by **Jennifer Buck**

Form a 4¼ x 5½-inch top-folded card from brown card stock. Center and adhere a 4 x 5¼-inch piece of Kosher Salt paper to card front. Adhere a 4¼ x 1-inch strip of Vegetable Broth paper to card front 1 inch above bottom edge. Staple decorative trim along bottom of Vegetable Broth paper.

Using Doodlecharms cartridge, cut dog bandana. Choose 3-inch size on dial. Load a 12 x 12-inch piece of Vegetable Broth paper into cutter. Press "<shift>," "<blackout>," "<doghse>" and "<cut>." Adhere bandana to lower left area of card front as shown with foam dots.

To cut dog, choose 3½-inch size on dial. Load a 12 x 12-inch piece of kraft card stock into cutter. Press "<dog>" and "<cut>." Repeat with brown card stock. Adhere kraft dog face to brown dog face.

To cut dog face pieces, choose 3½-inch size on dial. Load a 12 x 12-inch piece of brown card stock into cutter. Press "<shift>," "<dog>" and "<cut.>" Repeat with red card stock.

Adhere brown ear and eye piece to kraft dog face. Adhere red nose to dog face. Adhere googly eyes to kraft dog face. Adhere to card front as shown with foam dots.

For inside, cut a 4 x 5¼-inch piece of ivory card stock inside card. Using Plantin SchoolBook cartridge, cut blast. Choose 2¾-inch size on dial. Load a 12 x 12-inch piece of brown card stock into cutter. Press "<blast>" and "<cut>." Adhere to top of ivory rectangle.

Using Lyrical Letters cartridge, cut letters. Choose 1-inch size on dial. Load a 12 x 12-inch piece of ivory card stock into cutter. Press "<r>," "<u>," "<f>," "<f>," "<d>," "<a>" and "<y>." Press "<cut>."

To cut question mark, choose 1-inch size on dial. Load a 12 x 12-inch piece of ivory card stock into cutter. Press "<shift>," "<?>" and "<cut>." Adhere letters to brown blast inside card. ●

Sources: Card stock from Stampin' Up!; printed papers from Jillibean Soup; Cricut machine and cartridges from Provo Craft.

You Are Appreciated

Design by **Sherry Wright**

Form a 4¾ x 5¼-inch top-folded card from red card stock. Cut a piece of printed paper slightly smaller than card front; distress edges and adhere to card front. Using bright green ink, stamp Vintage Ledger onto white card stock; trim to 4 x 4½ inches. Distress edges and adhere to card front.

Using Home Accents cartridge, cut apple. Choose 4-inch size on dial and load a 5 x 5-inch piece of red card stock into cutter. Press "<apple>" and "<cut>."

Using red ink, stamp "You are appreciated" onto white card stock; cut out and ink edges red. Adhere apple and sentiment to card as shown.

Using bright green ink, stamp apple onto white card stock; cut out and color center heart red. Adhere to right side of card front as shown. Add gems. Slide binder clip onto upper left edge of card. ●

Sources: Card stock from Prism Papers; printed paper from October Afternoon; stamps from Cornish Heritage Farms; chalk ink pads from Clearsnap Inc.; gems from Queen & Co.; Cricut machine and cartridge from Provo Craft; Zip Dry Paper Glue from Beacon Adhesives Inc.

Materials

- Cricut Expression machine
- Cartridge: Home Accents (#29-0542)
- Card stock: red, white
- Detours Fruit Stand printed paper
- Stamps: Making the Grade set, Vintage Ledger
- Chalk ink pads: red, bright green
- Red marker
- 2 red flat-back gems
- Red binder clip
- Instant-dry paper glue

Get Better

Design by **Lynn Ghahary**

Using Indie Art cartridge, cut adhesive bandage. Choose 3-inch size on dial. Load a 4 x 6-inch piece of tan card stock. Press "<bandaid>" and "<cut>."

- - - - - - - - - - - - - - - - - - - -

To cut adhesive bandage shadow, choose 3-inch size on dial. Load a 4 x 6-inch piece of brown card stock into cutter. Press "<shadow>," "<bandaid>" and "<cut>."

- - - - - - - - - - - - - - - - - - - -

Using Graphically Speaking cartridge, cut hearts. Choose 1¼-inch size on dial. Load a 4 x 6-inch piece of red card stock into cutter. Press "<icon>," "<image02>" and "<cut>." Choose 3-inch size on dial. Load a 4 x 6-inch piece of red card stock into cutter. Press "<icon>," "<image02>" and "<cut>."

- - - - - - - - - - - - - - - - - - - -

Using Plantin SchoolBook cartridge, cut inside sentiment. Choose 1½-inch size on dial. Load a 6 x 12-inch piece of blue card stock into cutter. Press "<tallball>," "<soon>" and "<cut>."

- - - - - - - - - - - - - - - - - - - -

Using Tags, Bags, Boxes & More cartridge, cut tag. Choose ¾-inch size on dial. Load a 4 x 6-inch piece of ivory card stock into cutter. Press "<hole option>," "<lgcrc2>" and "<cut>."

- - - - - - - - - - - - - - - - - - - -

Form a 4½ x 5¾-inch side-folded card from kraft card stock. Cut two 4 x 1½-inch strips of Dirt Roads paper and adhere to top and bottom of a 4 x 5¼-inch piece of Gazebo paper. Distress edges. Machine-sew zigzag stitches along paper seams. Center and adhere to a 4¼ x 5½-inch piece of red card stock.

- - - - - - - - - - - - - - - - - - - -

Hand-print, or use a computer to generate, "better get better" on ivory tag; ink edges. Adhere to bottom of rectangle with foam dots.

- - - - - - - - - - - - - - - - - - - -

Thread hemp cord through one button and then through left hole of tag; wrap cord around back of red rectangle, through right hole of tag and through second button. Tie a knot. Trim ends. Center and adhere assembled rectangle to card front.

- - - - - - - - - - - - - - - - - - - -

Adhere tan adhesive bandage to brown shadow. Adhere small heart to adhesive bandage with foam dots. Adhere adhesive bandage to card front as shown. Adhere large heart inside card; adhere "soon" on top of heart. ●

- - - - - - - - - - - - - - - - - - - -

Sources: Card stock from Bazzill Basics Paper Inc., Doodlebug Design Inc. and Stampin' Up!; printed papers from October Afternoon; buttons from BasicGrey; Cricut machine and cartridges from Provo Craft.

Materials

- Cricut Expression machine
- Cartridges: Tags, Bags, Boxes & More (#29-0022), Indie Art (#29-0539), Graphically Speaking (#29-0590), Plantin SchoolBook (#29-0390)
- Card stock: blue, brown, kraft, red, tan, ivory
- Detours double-sided printed papers: Dirt Roads, Gazebo
- Tan ink pad
- Brown fine-tip pen
- Hemp cord
- 2 striped red buttons
- Sewing machine with white thread
- Adhesive foam dots
- Paper adhesive
- Computer and printer (optional)

Hang in There

Design by Kimber McGray

Using Wild Card cartridge, cut card base. Choose 5½-inch size on dial. Load a 6 x 12-inch piece of yellow card stock into cutter. Press "<tweety>" and "<cut>."

To cut branch, choose 5½-inch size on dial. Load a 6 x 12-inch piece of Brown Sugar paper into cutter. Press "<shift>," "<frame>," "<tweety>" and "<cut>."

To cut small bird, choose 5½-inch size on dial. Load a 6 x 12-inch piece of blue card stock into cutter. Press "<icon>," "<tweety>" and "<cut>." Press "<stop>" after bird is cut.

To cut sentiment, choose 5½-inch size on dial. Load 6 x 12-inch piece of blue card stock into cutter. Press "<shift>," "<phrase>," "<tweety>" and "<cut>."

To cut scrolled frame, choose 5½-inch size on dial. Load a 6 x 12-inch piece of Crown Brocade paper into cutter. Press "<frame>," "<tweety>" and "<cut>."

To cut large bird, choose 5½-inch size on dial. Load a 6 x 12-inch piece of Crown Brocade paper into cutter. Press "<shift>," <icon>," "<tweety>" and "<cut>."

Round corners of card. Adhere frame to lower right corner of card front with foam dots. Adhere small bird to end of branch; adhere branch to card front as shown with foam dots. Tie twine around frame opening and edge of card; trim ends. Adhere sentiment to lower right corner inside card. Adhere large bird next to sentiment. ●

Sources: Blue card stock from Core'dinations; embossed card stock from Bazzill Basics Paper Inc.; Just Chillin paper from Making Memories; Spicy Pumpkin paper and twine from Jillibean Soup; Cricut machine and cartridge from Provo Craft.

Materials

- Cricut Expression machine
- Cartridge: Wild Card (#29-0591)
- Card stock: blue, yellow embossed
- Printed papers: Just Chillin Boy Crown Brocade double-sided, Spicy Pumpkin Brown Sugar
- Twine
- Corner rounder
- Adhesive foam dots
- Paper adhesive

Owl Hello

Design by **Kimber McGray**

Using Wild Card cartridge, cut owl card base. Choose 4½-inch size on dial and load a 6 x 12-inch sheet of Kosher Salt paper into cutter. Press "<owl>" followed by "<cut>."

To cut owl eyes, choose 4½-inch size on dial and load a 6 x 6-inch piece of Vegetable Juice paper into cutter. Press "<liner>" and "<owl>." Press "<stop>" after circles are cut.

For owl inside, choose 4½-inch size on dial and load a 6 x 12-inch sheet of kraft paper into cutter. Press "<blackout>," "<owl>" and "<cut>."

For "Hello" sentiment, choose 4-inch size on dial and load a 4 x 6-inch piece of orange card stock into cutter. Press "<phrase>" followed by "<owl>." Press "<cut>." To assemble, adhere kraft paper piece inside card. Attach circles around eyes with foam tape. Adhere gems for eyes. Adhere sentiment inside. Outline sentiment with black pen. ●

Sources: Kraft paper and printed papers from Jillibean Soup; card stock from Core'dinations; gems from Zva Creative; Cricut machine and cartridge from Provo Craft.

Materials

- Cricut machine
- Cartridge: Wild Card (#29-0591)
- Orange card stock
- Double-sided printed papers: Lentil Soup Kosher Salt, Alphabet Soup Vegetable Juice
- Kraft paper
- 2 orange flat-back gems
- Black fine-tip pen
- Adhesive foam tape
- Paper adhesive

You Are So Sweet

Design by **Lynn Ghahary**

Using Indie Art cartridge, cut ice cream cone. Choose 7-inch size on dial. Load a 6 x 12-inch piece of light brown card stock into cutter. Press "<icecream>" and "<cut>."

To cut ice cream cone shadow, choose 7-inch size on dial. Load a 6 x 12-inch piece of dark brown card stock into cutter. Press "<shadow>," "<icecream>" and "<cut>."

To cut ice cream shadow, choose 7-inch size on dial. Load a 6 x 12-inch piece of pink card stock into cutter. Press "<shadow>," "<icecream>" and "<cut>."

To cut a second ice cream shadow, choose 7-inch size on dial. Load a 6 x 12-inch piece of pink card stock into cutter. Press "<shift>," "<shadow>," "<icecream>" and "<cut>."

To cut ice cream, choose 7-inch size on dial. Load a 6 x 12-inch piece of pink printed paper into cutter. Press "<shift>," "<icecream>" and "<cut>."

To assemble card, adhere light brown ice cream cone to dark brown ice cream cone shadow. Trim pink ice cream shadow so only top portion remains as shown. Adhere to top of dark brown ice cream cone shadow. Set aside.

For card front, adhere pink ice cream to pink ice cream shadow. Attach crystals. Place card front on top of dark brown ice cream cone and punch a 1/16-inch hole through center top. Fold green wire into thirds to increase thickness. Slip one end of wire through punched hole from front to back. Insert brad through hole securing end of wire with brad prongs. Add stickers and rub-on transfers inside card to complete the following sentiment: "YOU ARE SO SWEET ♥." ●

Sources: Card stock from Bazzill Basics Paper Inc., Doodlebug Design Inc. and Stampin' Up!; printed paper from G.C.D. Studios; large brad from Bazzill Basics Paper Inc.; wire from Making Memories; crystals from Martha Stewart Crafts; rub-on transfer from October Afternoon; Cricut machine and cartridge from Provo Craft.

Materials

- Cricut Expression machine
- Cartridge: Indie Art (#29-0539)
- Card stock: dark brown, light brown, pink
- Pink dots printed paper
- 6 inches green craft wire
- Self-adhesive crystals: pink, dark pink, clear
- "YOU ARE SO" rub-on transfer
- White glitter stickers to spell "SWEET ♥"
- Large red brad
- 1/16-inch hole punch
- Paper adhesive

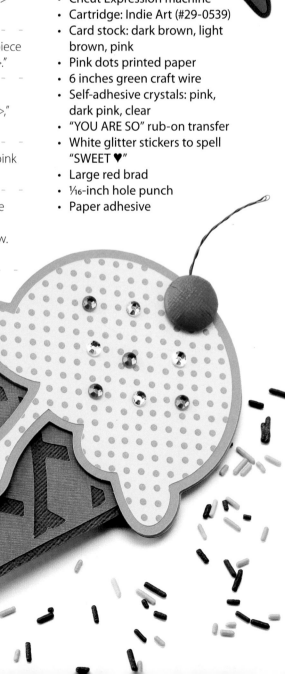

Sweet Girl

Design by **Lynn Ghahary**

Using Indie Art cartridge, cut strawberry card back. Choose 6½-inch size on dial. Load a 12 x 12-inch piece of green card stock into cutter. Press "<blackout>," "<strwbery>" and "<cut>." Repeat with a 12 x 12-inch piece of black card stock. This will be the base of the card front.

To cut strawberry card front, choose 6½-inch size on dial. Load a 12 x 12-inch piece of red printed paper into cutter. Press "<strwbery>" and "<cut>." Repeat with a 12 x 12-inch piece of green card stock.

Using Plantin SchoolBook cartridge, cut flower. Choose 1¼-inch size on dial. Load a 4 x 6-inch piece of white card stock into cutter. Press "<flower>" and "<cut>."

Using Graphically Speaking cartridge, cut inside sentiment. Choose 5½-inch size on dial. Load a 6 x 12-inch piece of red printed paper into cutter. Press "<shift>," "<image13>" and "<cut>."

Materials
- Cricut Expression machine
- Cartridges: Indie Art (#29-0539), Graphically Speaking (#29-0590), Plantin SchoolBook (#29-0390)
- Card stock: green, black, white
- Red printed paper
- 18 inches ⅜-inch-wide black gingham ribbon
- Twine
- Yellow round button
- Sewing machine with white thread
- Paper adhesive

To assemble the card front, machine-stitch around edge of red strawberry. Adhere red strawberry to black strawberry. Cut off leaves from green strawberry and adhere at top of card front. Score card front just below green leaves. Adhere card front to card back at top portion only. Tie ribbon around top of strawberry and tie a bow; trim ends. Tie a small piece of twine around ribbon bow; trim ends. Thread another piece of twine through button; tie a knot on back and trim ends. Adhere button to flower; adhere to ribbon bow. Adhere sentiment inside card. ●

Sources: Card stock from Bazzill Basics Paper Inc. and Stampin' Up!; printed paper from G.C.D. Studios; Cricut machine and cartridges from Provo Craft.

HB2U

Design by **Lynn Ghahary**

Using Graphically Speaking cartridge, cut car base. Choose 5½-inch size on dial. Load a 6 x 12-inch piece of gray card stock into cutter. Press "<icon blackout>," "<image21>" and "<cut>."

To cut car body, choose 5½-inch size on dial. Load a 6 x 12-inch piece of gray card stock into cutter. Press "<icon blackout>," "<image21>" and "<cut>."

Cut another car body by choosing 5½-inch size on dial and loading a 6 x 12-inch piece of blue card stock into cutter. Press "<icon>," "<image21>" and "<cut>."

To cut car tires, choose 2-inch size on dial. Load a 4 x 6-inch piece of gray card stock into cutter. Press "<shift>," "<icon blackout>," "<image21>" and "<cut>."

To cut car tires, choose 2-inch size on dial. Load a 4 x 6-inch piece of black card stock. Press "<shift>," "<icon>," "<image 21>" and "<cut>."

To cut license plate, choose 2-inch size on dial. Load a 4 x 6-inch piece of white card stock. Press "<shift>," "<icon blackout>," "<image21>" and "<cut>."

To cut headlights, choose ¾-inch size on dial. Load a 4 x 6-inch piece of yellow card stock into cutter. Press "<shift>," "<image23>" and "<cut>." Repeat.

To cut inside sentiment, choose 2-inch size on dial. Load a 6 x 12-inch piece of blue card stock into cutter. Press "<type>," "<image30>" and "<cut>."

Adhere blue car body to gray car body. Adhere black car tires to gray car tires. Adhere car tires to car body adhering them to back of car body as shown.

Apply glitter to headlights. Adhere on top of brads. Punch a ¹⁄₁₆-inch hole through sides of car body where headlights will be attached. Place additional gray car body behind assembled car body and repunch hole through left side of car. This is where card will be "hinged." Insert brads through holes.

Hand-print, or use a computer to generate, "HB2U" onto white license plate. Adhere to card front as shown. Adhere sentiment inside card. ●

Sources: Card stock from Die Cuts With A View and Stampin' Up!; glitter from Doodlebug Design Inc.; large brads from Queen & Co.; Cricut machine and cartridge from Provo Craft.

Materials

- Cricut Expression machine
- Cartridge: Graphically Speaking (#29-0590)
- Card stock: blue, gray, black, white, yellow
- Chunky yellow glitter
- 2 large green brads
- Black fine-tip pen
- ¹⁄₁₆-inch hole punch
- Paper adhesive
- Computer and printer (optional)

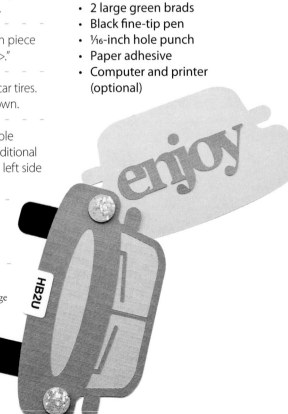

4 You

Design by **Lynn Ghahary**

Using Plantin SchoolBook catridge, cut star card base. Choose 6-inch size on dial. Load a 6 x 12-inch piece of printed paper into cutter. Press "<star>" and "<cut>."

To cut a star, choose 6-inch size on dial. Load a 6 x 12-inch piece of yellow card stock into cutter. Press "<shadow>," "<star>" and "<cut>." Repeat for a second yellow star.

To cut "4", choose 2½-inch size on dial. Load a 4 x 6-inch piece of red card stock into cutter. Press "<shadow>," "<4>" and "<cut>."

To cut sentiment, choose 1¼-inch size on dial. Load a 6 x 6-inch piece of red card stock into cutter. Press "<star>" and "<cut>."

Using Opposites Attract cartridge, cut "you." Choose 2-inch size on dial. Load a 4 x 6-inch piece of dark blue card stock into cutter. Press "<upright>," "<you>" and "<cut>."

Assemble card. Adhere blue star to yellow star. Adhere red "4" centered on blue star; adhere "you" on top of "4." Place this star on top of second yellow star and punch a ¹⁄₁₆-inch hole through top; insert brad. Attach more brads to card front. Adhere "star" inside card. ●

Sources: Card stock from Bazzill Basics Paper Inc.; printed paper from G.C.D. Studios; Cricut machine and cartridges from Provo Craft.

Materials
- Cricut Expression machine
- Cartridges: Plantin SchoolBook (#29-0390), Opposites Attract (#29-0227)
- Card stock: dark blue, red, yellow
- Lost in Paradise Pool Tiles double-sided printed paper
- Star brads in assorted colors
- ¹⁄₁₆-inch hole punch
- Paper adhesive

Wishing You ...

Design by **Sherry Wright**

Using Storybook cartridge, cut large butterfly. Choose 6-inch size on dial. Load a 7 x 7-inch piece of printed paper into cutter. Press "<shadow>," "<butrfly2>" and "<cut>." Ink edges and set aside.

To cut small butterfly, choose 4½-inch size on dial. Load a 6 x 6-inch piece of pink card stock into cutter. Press "<shadow>," "<butrfly2>" and "<cut>." Ink edges and adhere to large butterfly.

To cut circle, choose 1¾-inch size on dial. Load a 3 x 3-inch piece of white card stock into cutter. Press "<accent blackout>," "<branch3>" and "<cut>."

Apply rub-on transfer to white circle. Adhere to small butterfly. Add gems on each side of circle.

Form a 6 x 6½-inch top-folded card from pink card stock. Place butterfly on card front positioning tips of wings ⅛ inch from top edge. Adhere butterfly in place and trim around butterfly leaving a ⅛-inch border. Do not cut folds at tips of wings. ●

Sources: Card stock from Core'dinations; printed paper from SEI; gems from Queen & Co.; rub-on transfer from Heart & Home Inc./ Melissa Frances; chalk ink pad from Clearsnap Inc.; Cricut machine and cartridge from Provo Craft; Zip Dry Paper Glue from Beacon Adhesives Inc.

Materials

- Cricut Expression machine
- Cartridge: Storybook (#29-0589)
- Card stock: pink, white
- White/pink printed paper
- 2 flat-back pink gems
- Happy Birthday-themed rub-on transfer
- Dusty pink chalk ink pad
- Instant-dry paper glue

Special Thanks

Design by **Kimber McGray**

Materials

- Cricut machine
- Cartridges: Accent Essentials (#29-0391), Walk in My Garden (#29-0223)
- Card stock: green, yellow
- Double-sided printed papers: Soup Staples Olive Sugar, Urban Prairie Patchwork Quilt, Urban Prairie Petticoat
- Light brown chalk ink pad
- Yellow brad
- Straight pin
- Adhesive foam tape
- Paper adhesive

Using Accent Essentials cartridge, cut flower card front. Choose 5-inch size on dial and load a 6 x 12-inch piece of Patchwork Quilt paper into cutter. Press "<Shift>," "<accent46>" and "<cut>." Load a 6 x 12-inch piece of Prairie Petticoat paper into cutter and choose 5-inch size on dial. Press "<accent46>" and "<cut>."

For flower card base, choose 5-inch size on dial and load a 6 x 12-inch piece of green card stock into cutter. Press "<shadow>," "<shift>," "<accent46>" and "<cut>."

For leaves, choose 2-inch size on dial and load a 6 x 12-inch piece of Olive Sugar paper into cutter. Press "<shift>" and "<accent42>." Press "<accent42>" to create a second leaf. Press "<cut>."

Using Walk in My Garden cartridge, cut sentiment by choosing 1-inch size on dial and loading a 4 x 6-inch piece of yellow card stock into cutter. Press "<shift>," "<thanks>" and "<cut>."

Ink edges of all pieces. Assemble card. Lay yellow flower on green flower; poke small hole through a petal with pin and insert brad to attach flowers. Adhere pink flower ring with foam tape. Flower ring will cover brad.

Adhere center pink flower with foam tape. Attach green leaves to back of yellow flower. Adhere sentiment inside card. ●

Sources: Card stock from Core'dinations; Soup Staples paper from Jillibean Soup; Urban Prairie papers from BasicGrey; chalk ink pad from Clearsnap Inc.; Cricut machine and cartridges from Provo Craft.

For Your New Home

Design by **Jennifer Buck**

Using Wild Card cartridge, cut house card base. Choose 7-inch size on dial. Load a 12 x 12-inch piece of white card stock. Press "<house>," "<blackout>" and "<cut>." Fold card at score marks.

To cut house layers, choose 7-inch size on dial. Load a 12 x 12-inch piece of kraft gingham paper into cutter. Press "<house>" and "<cut>." Repeat three more times, once with black card stock, once with red card stock and once with light blue polka-dot paper.

Cut out front of gingham house and adhere to white card front. Sponge yellow and orange inks inside window for light. Cut out roof from light blue house and adhere to card front. Cut out chimney and window frame from black house and adhere in place. Cut out door from red house and adhere. Add silver ball for doorknob.

To cut two trees, choose 7-inch size on dial. Load a 12 x 12-inch piece of olive green card stock into cutter. Press "<icon>," "<house>" and "<cut>." Repeat three more times with olive green card stock and four times with kraft card stock. Cut off tops of olive green trees. Layer and adhere two olive green trees on top of two kraft trees using dimensional dots. Cut off bottoms of remaining two kraft trees; adhere on top of two other kraft trees. Adhere to card front as shown.

For inside, cut a 3¼ x 2-inch piece of kraft card stock; punch scallops along top edge. Adhere a 3¼ x 1½-inch piece of gingham paper to scallop piece. Adhere inside card ½ inch above bottom edge.

To cut sentiment, choose 7-inch size on dial. Load a 12 x 12-inch piece of black card stock into cutter. Press "<shift>," "<house>," "<phrase>" and "<cut>." Adhere inside card. ●

Sources: Card stock, printed paper and scallop border punch from Stampin' Up!; silver ball from Kaisercraft; Cricut machine and cartridge from Provo Craft.

Materials

- Cricut Expression machine
- Cartridge: Wild Card (#29-0591)
- Card stock: white, black, red, olive green, kraft
- Printed papers: kraft gingham, light blue polka-dot
- Pigment ink pads: yellow, orange
- Silver self-adhesive ball
- Scallop border punch
- Craft sponge
- Adhesive dimensional dots
- Paper adhesive

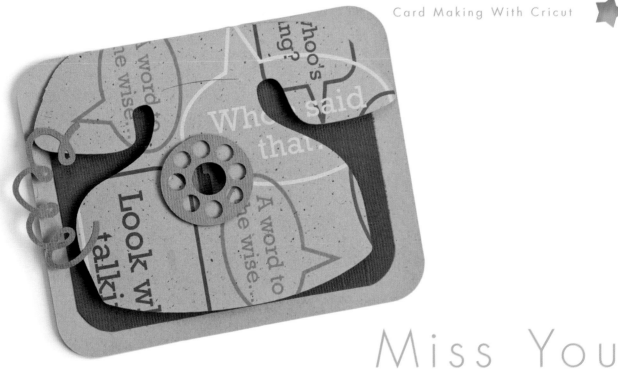

Miss You

Design by **Kimber McGray**

Materials
- Cricut machine
- Cartridge: Wild Card (#29-0591)
- Card stock: brown, green
- Talk Soup Bit of Babble printed kraft paper
- Corner rounder
- Adhesive foam tape
- Paper adhesive

Using Wild Card cartridge, cut phone card base. Choose 5½-inch size on dial and load a 6 x 12-inch piece of printed paper into cutter. Press "<Hello>" and then "<cut>."

For phone dial, choose 5½-inch size on cutter dial and load a 6 x 12-inch sheet of green card stock into cutter. Press "<liner>." Press "<Hello>" followed by "<cut>."

Continue on same piece of green card stock already loaded to cut cord. Press "<icon>," "<Hello>" and then "<cut>."

Continue on same piece of green card stock already loaded to cut sentiment. Press "<phrase>," "<Hello>" and "<cut>."

To assemble, adhere dial to card front with foam tape. Adhere cord to card front. Cut a 4¾ x 3⅝-inch piece of brown card stock; round corners and adhere inside card. Adhere sentiment inside card. ●

Sources: Card stock from Core'dinations; printed paper from Jillibean Soup; Cricut machine and cartridge from Provo Craft.

Wedding Congrats

Design by **Kimber McGray**

Using Wild Card cartridge, cut wedding cake card base. Choose 5½-inch size on dial and load a 6 x 12-inch piece of printed paper into cutter. Press "<cake>" followed by "<cut>."

For wedding cake card inside, choose 5½-inch size on dial and load a 6 x 12-inch piece of light blue card stock into cutter. Press "<blackout>," "<cake>" and "<cut>."

For "Congrats" sentiment, choose 5½-inch size on dial and load a 6 x 6-inch piece of printed paper into cutter. Press "<shift>," "<phrase>," "<#1>" and "<cut>."

To assemble card, adhere light blue card stock inside card. Add pearls to card front. Wrap ribbon around card front and tie into a bow. Trim ends. Add stick pins to bow. Adhere sentiment inside card. ●

Sources: Card stock from Core'dinations; printed paper from Jillibean Soup; ribbon from Creative Impressions; pearls from Zva Creative; stick pins from Fancy Pants Designs; Cricut machine and cartridge from Provo Craft.

Materials
- Cricut machine
- Cartridge: Wild Card (#29-0591)
- Light blue card stock
- Soup Staples White Macaroni double-sided printed paper
- 20 inches ½-inch-wide white satin ribbon
- Self-adhesive pearls
- Heart stick pins: 1 blue, 1 pink
- Paper adhesive

Love You

Design by **Melissa Phillips**

Materials

- Cricut Expression machine
- Cartridge: Wild Card (#29-0591)
- Pink card stock
- Printed papers: pink striped, pink floral, white flocked
- Ticket die cut
- Chipboard shapes: pink heart, "Y," "U"
- White self-adhesive pearls
- Silk flower
- 16 inches ½-inch-wide white satin ribbon
- White string
- Pink glitter
- Pink glimmer spray
- Brown dye ink pad
- ⅛-inch hole punch
- Sewing machine with tan thread
- Paper adhesive

Using Wild Card cartridge, cut heart card. Choose 4½-inch size on dial. Load a 12 x 12-inch piece of pink card stock into cutter. Press "<heart>," "<blackout>" and "<cut>."

To cut heart frame, choose 3¼-inch size on dial. Load a 12 x 12-inch piece of pink striped paper into cutter. Press "<heart>," "<frame>" and "<cut>."

Trace heart card onto pink floral paper; cut out and ink edges. Adhere to front of heart card. Adhere a piece of white flocked paper to back of heart frame covering opening. Ink edges of heart frame and adhere to card front as shown. Machine-sew zigzag stitches along edges of heart frame.

Apply glitter to chipboard letters and spray with glimmer spray. Let dry. Adhere letters and small heart to card front as shown. Embellish heart with pearls. Wrap ribbon around card front and tie a bow; trim ends. Punch a ⅛-inch hole through left end of ticket; tie ticket onto ribbon bow with string. Trim ends. Adhere flower to ribbon bow; add pearl to flower center. ●

Sources: Card stock from Prism Papers; printed papers from Cosmo Cricket, Doodlebug Design Inc. and October Afternoon; chipboard shapes from Tattered Angels and Heidi Swapp/Advantus; self-adhesive pearls from Zva Creative; ticket from Making Memories; glitter from Doodlebug Design Inc.; glimmer spray from Tattered Angels; Cricut machine and cartridge from Provo Craft.

Sweet Baby Girl

Design by **Sherry Wright**

Using Storybook cartridge, cut card. Choose 6-inch size on dial. Load an 8 x 8-inch piece of blue card stock into cutter. Press "<shift>," "<accent blackout>," "<wishtrue>" and "<cut>." Fold in half and repeat all steps with Trailing Vines paper. Cut polka-dot card in half; ink edges of one half and adhere to front of blue card.

To cut circle, choose 2½-inch size on dial. Load a 3 x 3-inch piece of white card stock into cutter. Press "<accent blackout>," "<branch3>" and "<cut>." Ink edges and adhere to card front as shown.

Using Stretch your Imagination cartridge, cut baby carriage. Choose 2½-inch size on dial. Load a 3 x 3-inch piece of Flower Fair paper into cutter. Press "<shift>," "<silhouette>," "<bbybgy>" and "<cut>." Adhere to right side of white circle.

Using Graphically Speaking cartridge, choose ¾-inch size on dial. Load a 2 x 2-inch piece of Trailing Vines paper into cutter. Press "<type>," "<image13>" and "<cut>." Adhere to white circle overlapping baby carriage. Apply "sweet" rub-on transfer above "girl." Attach gems to baby carriage.

Wrap ribbon around left side of card front and tie a bow; trim ends with pinking shears. ●

Sources: Card stock from Prism Papers; printed papers and rub-on transfer from Dream Street Papers; gems from Queen & Co.; chalk ink pad from Clearsnap Inc.; Cricut machine and cartridges from Provo Craft.

Materials

- Cricut Expression machine
- Cartridges: Storybook (#29-0589), Stretch your Imagination (#29-0422), Graphically Speaking (#29-0590)
- Card stock: blue, white
- Nature's Poetry double-sided printed papers: Trailing Vines, Flower Fair
- "sweet" rub-on transfer
- 3 pink flat-back gems
- 18 inches ⅞-inch-wide white satin ribbon
- Brown chalk ink pad
- Pinking shears
- Paper glue

Love

Design by **Kandis Smith**

Materials

- Cricut Expression machine
- Cartridge: Wedding (#29-0544)
- Card stock: pink, kraft
- Printed papers: pink floral, brown striped, white/pink
- Small envelope
- "LOVE" stamp
- Ink pads: tan, brown
- Flat-back self-adhesive pearls
- 2 pink paper flowers
- 2 red flat-back gems
- 4 inches ⅞-inch-wide brown satin ribbon
- Punches: ¾-inch circle, ¼-inch hole
- Sewing machine with brown thread
- Paper adhesive

Form a 5½ x 5½-inch top-folded card from pink card stock. Center and adhere a 5 x 5-inch piece of pink floral printed paper to card front. Machine-sew zigzag stitches along edges of printed paper.

Cut a 4½ x 3-inch rectangle from kraft card stock; trim left corners at an angle to form a tag. Ink edges tan. Punch a ¾-inch circle from pink floral printed paper; adhere to left end of tag. Punch a ¼-inch hole through circle. Tie ribbon through hole into a knot; trim ends into V-notches. Adhere flowers to ribbon knot; adhere gems to flower centers. Stamp "LOVE" on lower left edge of tag with brown ink. Adhere to card front as shown.

Using Wedding cartridge, cut scallop heart. Choose 3-inch size on dial. Load a 12 x 12-inch piece of brown striped paper into cutter. Press "<scallop heart>" and "<cut>."

To cut inside heart, choose 3-inch size on dial. Load a 12 x 12-inch piece of white/pink printed paper into cutter. Press "<shift>," "<scallop heart>" and "<cut>."

Slide money or a gift card into small envelope; adhere to back of heart. Adhere to card front as shown. Accent heart with pearls. ●

Sources: Card stock from Core'dinations; printed papers from SEI; stamp from Hero Arts; Cricut machine and cartridge from Provo Craft.

Happy Shopping

Design by **Kimber McGray**

Form a 5½ x 4¼-inch top-folded card from kraft paper. Draw stitches along edges using gel pen.

Using Wild Card cartridge, cut piggy bank. Choose 3½-inch size on dial and load a 6 x 12-inch piece of printed paper into cutter. Press "<shift>," "<frame>" and "<real dial size>." Press "<GiftCard>" and "<cut>."

For "Happy $hopping" sentiment, choose 2-inch size on dial and load a 4 x 6-inch piece of black card stock into cutter. Press "<phrase>," "<all in one>" and "<cut>."

Attach piggy bank to card front with foam tape. Adhere sentiment to piggy bank. ●

Materials
- Cricut machine
- Cartridge: Wild Card (#29-0591)
- Black card stock
- Kraft paper
- Soup Staples Pink Sugar double-sided printed paper
- White gel pen
- Adhesive foam tape
- Paper adhesive

Sources: Black card stock from Core'dinations; kraft paper and printed paper from Jillibean Soup; Cricut machine and cartridge from Provo Craft.

BIG Day

Design by **Kimber McGray**

Cut a 7 x 8½-inch piece of printed paper. With short side horizontal, score horizontal lines 1½ inches and 5 inches above bottom edge. Fold up bottom flap and adhere short sides to create a pocket. Fold down top flap and round bottom corners on top flap.

Using Graphically Speaking cartridge, cut number border. Choose 2-inch size on dial. Load a 12 x 12-inch piece of red card stock into cutter. Press "<icon>," "<image27>" and "<cut>."

To cut BIG sentiment, choose 2½-inch size on dial. Continue on same piece of card stock. Press "<image05>" and "<cut>." **Note:** *Use just the letters "BIG" cut from image.*

To cut star, choose 3½-inch size on dial. Load a 6 x 12-inch piece of yellow card stock into cutter. Press "<shift>," "<icon>," "<image16>" and "<cut>."

To cut day sentiment, choose 2½-inch size on dial. Continue on same piece of card stock. Press "<shift>," "<word>" and "<cut>."

Materials
- Cricut Expression machine
- Cartridge: Graphically Speaking (#29-0590)
- Card stock: red, yellow
- Soup Staples White Stock printed paper
- Corner rounder
- Adhesive foam dots
- Paper adhesive

Adhere star to card front. Adhere number border to card front using foam dots. Adhere "BIG" centered inside card on bottom flap; adhere "day" to bottom flap overlapping "G." ●

Sources: Card stock from Core'dinations; printed paper from Jillibean Soup; Cricut machine and cartridge from Provo Craft.

Thanks

Design by **Kimber McGray**

Using Wild Card cartridge, cut trifold card base. Choose 7-inch size on dial. Load a 12 x 12-inch piece of printed paper into cutter. Press "<trifold>" and "<cut>."

To cut frame, choose 7-inch size on dial. Continue on same piece of printed paper. Press "<frame>," "<trifold>" and "<cut>."

To cut thanks sentiment, choose 1½-inch size on dial. Continue on same piece of printed paper. Press "<phrase>," "<quotes>," "<flip>" and "<cut>."

Fold card. Open card and cut along last fold line 2¼ inches down; cut across last panel at an angle. Refold card. Adhere frame around square opening on front panel. Adhere sentiment to card front as shown. ●

Sources: Printed paper from Pebbles Inc.; Cricut machine and cartridge from Provo Craft.

Materials
- Cricut Expression machine
- Cartridge: Wild Card (#29-0591)
- Lil' Miss Sister double-sided printed paper
- Paper adhesive

Teacher Gift Card

Design by **Jennifer Buck**

Using Wild Card cartridge, cut gift card holder. Choose 4-inch size on dial. Load a 12 x 12-inch piece of kraft card stock into cutter. Press "<booklet>" and "<cut>." Fold along scored lines

Adhere a 4 x ½-inch piece of gingham paper to front panel of gift card holder ¾ inch above bottom edge. Place ribbon along bottom of gingham strip and fold left end under creating a loop. Staple ribbon in place.

Using Home Accents cartridge, cut apple base. Choose 2-inch size on dial. Load a 12 x 12-inch piece of red card stock into cutter. Press "<blackout>," "<apple>" and "<cut>."

To cut remaining sections of apple, choose 2-inch size on dial. Load a 12 x 12-inch piece of black card stock into cutter. Press "<apple>" and "<cut>." Repeat with ivory card stock, olive green card stock and light tan card stock.

Remove centers from inner part of ivory apple and adhere to inner part of black apple. Punch out light tan apple centers and adhere to inner part of ivory apple. Adhere to red apple base. Adhere apple and olive green stem to front of card holder as shown using foam dots.

Fold up front panel of card holder and adhere a 4 x ½-inch strip of gingham paper to front of second panel. Using George and Basic Shapes cartridge, cut sentiment. Choose 1-inch size on dial. Load a 12 x 12-inch piece of black card stock into cutter. Press "<for you>" and "<cut>." Adhere to second panel.

Open gift card holder. Cut a 3¾ x 2¾-inch piece of gingham paper; round corners. Adhere centered inside card holder. Hand-stitch cross-stitches along sides of paper. ●

Materials

- Cricut Expression machine
- Cartridges: Wild Card (#29-0591), George and Basic Shapes (#29-0025), Home Accents (#29-0542)
- Card stock: black, ivory, light tan, red, olive green, kraft
- Kraft gingham printed paper
- 5 inches ¼-inch-wide black gingham ribbon
- Black thread
- Sewing needle
- Stapler
- Adhesive foam dots
- Paper adhesive

Sources: Card stock, printed paper and ribbon from Stampin' Up!; Cricut machine and cartridges from Provo Craft.

Super Star

Design by **Kimber McGray**

Using Wild Card cartridge, cut tri-fold card base. Choose 4-inch size on dial. Load a 6 x 12-inch piece of striped paper into cutter. Press "<blackout>," "<booklet>" and "<cut>."

For sentiment, choose 4-inch size on dial. Load a 6 x 12-inch piece of green card stock into cutter. Press "<phrase>," "<booklet>" and "<cut>."

For red stars, choose 4-inch size on dial and load a 6 x 12-inch piece of red stars paper into cutter. Press "<shift>," "<icon>," "<#1>" and "<cut>."

Using Plantin SchoolBook cartridge, cut orange star. Choose 3-inch size on dial. Load a 6 x 6-inch piece of orange paper. Press "<star>" and "<cut>."

To assemble card, score and fold card. Cut a horizontal slit across last panel 1½ inches from bottom edge to create pocket for gift card. Fold last panel inside and adhere edges.

Adhere orange star to front of card holder; outline with black pen. Adhere green sentiment to star. Adhere red stars with foam tape as shown. Punch a ⅛-inch hole through right side of all layers; tie ribbon through hole. Trim ends. ●

Sources: Card stock from Core'dinations; printed papers from Making Memories; ribbon from May Arts; Cricut machine and cartridges from Provo Craft.

Materials
- Cricut machine
- Cartridges: Plantin SchoolBook (#29-0390), Wild Card (#29-0591)
- Green card stock
- Printed papers: multicolored striped/orange, red stars
- 10 inches ⅛-inch-wide orange stitched ribbon
- Black fine-tip pen
- ⅛-inch hole punch
- Craft knife
- Adhesive foam tape
- Paper adhesive

Enjoy

Design by **Kimber McGray**

Materials

- Cricut machine
- Cartridges: Walk in My Garden (#29-0223), Wild Card (#29-0591)
- Red card stock
- Early Bird Cherry Pie double-sided printed paper
- Buttons: 1 blue, 1 red
- Twine
- Paper adhesive

Using Walk in My Garden cartridge, cut scallop card base. Choose 4-inch size on dial and load a 6 x 12-inch piece of printed paper into cutter. Press "<shift>," "<breadtag>," "<fldcrd>" and "<cut>."

Using Wild Card cartridge, cut sentiment by choosing 4-inch size on dial and loading a 4 x 6-inch piece of red card stock into cutter. Press "<phrase>," "<branch>" and "<cut>."

To assemble card, score and fold scallop card base. Adhere a ½ x 3-inch strip of red card stock to front of card holder as shown. Trim ends even. Tie twine around card front; thread twine through buttons and tie a bow. Trim ends. Adhere sentiment to right side of card holder. ●

Sources: Card stock from Core'dinations; printed paper from Cosmo Cricket; buttons from Making Memories; twine from Jillibean Soup; Cricut machine and cartridges from Provo Craft.

Birthday Girl

Design by **Sherry Wright**

Form a 5 x 5½-inch top-folded card from pink card stock. Set aside. Cut a 5 x 5½-inch piece of Gladys Pauline paper; ink edges. This will be card base. Cut a 4 x 5½-inch piece of Virginia Ruth paper; ink edges and adhere to card base ¾ inch from left edge.

Using Tags, Bags, Boxes & More cartridge, cut envelope. Choose 6-inch size on dial. Load a 12 x 12-inch piece of Gladys Pauline paper into cutter. Press "<tagkt1>" and "<cut>." Fold envelope; ink edges and adhere to base as shown. Thread ribbon through hole in envelope and around card base; tie a bow on top of envelope. Trim ends with pinking shears.

To cut circle, use Tags, Bags, Boxes & More cartridge. Choose 2½-inch size on dial. Load a 4 x 4-inch piece of pink card stock into cutter. Press "<shift>," "<circle-h>" and "<cut>." Ink edges and adhere to card front as shown.

Using Storybook cartridge, cut sentiment. Choose 2-inch size on dial. Load a 4 x 4-inch piece of Virginia Ruth paper into cutter. Press "<shift>," "<fancy/corner>," "<bdaygirl>" and "<cut>." Adhere to pink circle. Add gems. Adhere assembled card base to card front. ●

Materials

- Cricut Expression machine
- Cartridges: Storybook (#29-0589), Tags, Bags, Boxes & More (#29-0022)
- Pink card stock
- Forever Family double-sided printed papers: Gladys Pauline, Virginia Ruth
- Brown chalk ink pad
- 2 pink flat-back gems
- 20 inches ⅝-inch-wide ivory satin ribbon
- Pinking shears
- Instant-dry paper glue

Sources: Card stock from Core'dinations; printed papers from Dream Street Papers; gems from Queen & Co.; chalk ink pad from Clearsnap Inc.; Cricut machine and cartridges from Provo Craft; Zip Dry Paper Glue from Beacon Adhesives Inc.

Buyer's Guide

Adornit/Carolee's Creations
(435) 563-1100
www.adornit.com

American Crafts Inc.
(801) 226-0747
www.americancrafts.com

BasicGrey
(801) 544-1116
www.basicgrey.com

Bazzill Basics Paper Inc.
(800) 560-1610
www.bazzillbasics.com

Beacon Adhesives Inc.
(914) 699-3405
www.beaconcreates.com

Clearsnap Inc.
(888) 448-4862
www.clearsnap.com

Core'dinations
www.coredinations.com

Cornish Heritage Farms
(877) 860-5328
www.cornishheritagefarms.com

Cosmo Cricket
(800) 852-8810
www.cosmocricket.com

Creative Impressions
(719) 596-4860
www.creativeimpressions.com

Die Cuts With A View
(801) 224-6766
www.diecutswithaview.com

Doodlebug Design Inc.
www.doodlebugdesign.
homestead.com

Dream Street Papers
(480) 275-9736
www.dreamstreetpapers.com

Dress It Up
www.dressitup.com

Fancy Pants Designs
(801) 779-3212
www.fancypantsdesigns.com

Fiskars
(866) 348-5661
www.fiskarscrafts.com

Flower Soft Inc.
(877) 989-0205
www.flower-soft.com

G.C.D. Studios
(877) 272-0262
www.gcdstudios.com

Graphic 45
(866) 573-4806
www.g45papers.com

**Heart & Home Inc./
Melissa Frances**
(484) 248-6080
www.melissafrances.com

Heidi Swapp/Advantus
(904) 482-0092
www.heidiswapp.com

Hero Arts
(800) 822-4376
www.heroarts.com

Jillibean Soup
(888) 212-1177
www.jillibean-soup.com

K&Company
(800) 794-5866
www.kandcompany.com

Kaisercraft
(888) 684-7147
www.kaisercraft.net

Making Memories
(800) 286-5263
www.makingmemories.com

Martha Stewart Crafts
www.marthastewartcrafts.com

May Arts
(203) 637-8366
www.mayarts.com

me & my BIG ideas
(949) 583-2065
www.meandmybigideas.com

My Mind's Eye
(800) 665-5116
www.mymindseye.com

October Afternoon
(866) 513-5553
www.octoberafternoon.com

Papertrey Ink
www.papertreyink.com

Pebbles Inc.
(800) 438-8153
www.pebblesinc.com

Prism Papers
(866) 902-1002
www.prismpapers.com

Provo Craft
(800) 937-7686
www.provocraft.com

Queen & Co.
www.queenandco.com

Ranger Industries Inc.
(732) 389-3535
www.rangerink.com

SEI
(800) 333-3279
www.shopsei.com

Stampin' Up!
(800) STAMP UP (782-6787)
www.stampinup.com

Tattered Angels
(970) 622-9444
www.mytatteredangels.com

Webster's Pages
(800) 543-6104
www.websterspages.com

WorldWin Papers
(888) 843-6455
www.worldwinpapers.com

Zva Creative
(801) 243-9281
www.zvacreative.com

The Buyer's Guide listings are provided
as a service to our readers and should not
be considered an endorsement from this
publication.